# NORFOLK

## Wit & Humour

REBECCA SCARROW

BRADWELL
**BOOKS**

Published by Bradwell Books
9 Orgreave Close Sheffield S13 9NP
Email: books@bradwellbooks.co.uk
Compiled by Rebecca Scarrow

British Library Cataloguing in Publication Data: a catalogue record for
this book is available from the British Library.

1st Edition

ISBN: 9781909914124

Print: Gomer Press, Llandysul, Ceredigion SA44 4JL
Design by: jenksdesign@yahoo.co.uk
Illustrations: ©Tim O'Brien 2013

**A Norfolk farmer** once visited a farmer in Suffolk. The Norfolk farmer asked "How big is your farm?" to which the other man replied "Can you see those trees over there? That's the boundary of my farmland"

The farmer responded, "Wow. It takes me three days to drive to the boundary of my farm."

The man said "I had a car like that once."

**A rather cocky** man working on a busy construction site in Diss was bragging that he could outdo anyone in a feat of strength. He made a special case of making fun of Morris, one of the more senior workmen. After several minutes, Morris had had enough.

"Why don't you put your money where your mouth is?" he said. "I'll bet a week's wages that I can haul something in a wheelbarrow over to that outbuilding that you won't be able to wheel back."

"You're on, mate," the over confident young man replied. "It's a bet! Let's see what you got."

Morris reached out and grabbed the wheelbarrow by the handles. Then, nodding to the young man, he said, "All right. Get in."

**One day, a father** and his son arrived at the rugby ground to watch Thetford play Newmarket. But the man suddenly realised that he couldn't find their tickets for the game. He said to his son, "Nip home and see if I left the tickets there." And the boy answered "No probs, Dad." Half an hour later, he returned to his dad who was patiently waiting outside the football pitch and said, "Yep, they're on the kitchen table where you left them."

**A man went** to the doctor one day and said: "I've just been playing rugby for Harwich and when I got back, I found that when I touched my legs, my arms, my head, my tummy and everywhere else, it really hurt." So the doctor said: "Yes, that's because you've broken your finger."

## Unusual Norfolk place names

Cat's Common

Cannon Hoare Road

Clipbush Lane

Feltwell

Great Snoring

Hooker Road

Little Snoring

Slutshole Lane

Two Mile Bottom

Wormegay

**"I went to see** The Specials in Norfolk."

"Diss Town?"

"Is coming like a Ghost Town, yeah."

**A priest was** visiting Norfolk and while taking a trip along the coast he looked out to sea where two local rugby supporters were out in a boat. Suddenly he noticed that in the water, a Woodbridge rugby fan was being attacked by a shark. Fortunately, the Norfolk fans arrived in a boat and pulled the Woodbridge fan to safety, killed the shark and pulled it onto the boat.

The priest beckoned the boat to the shore and said "I've never seen anything so brave. I understood that there was intense rivalry between Norfolk and Suffolk rugby fans but that has restored my faith in mankind". He then blessed the Norfolk men and left.

One of the locals turned to his friend and asked "What was he on about?"

"Dunno" said his mate "But he knows nothing about shark fishing. Do we need any fresh bait?"

**The Seven Dwarves** were walking through the forest one day when they suddenly fell into a deep ravine. Snow White, who was following along behind her friends, stared over the edge of the ravine and called out to the dwarfs. From the very depths of the dark hole a voice came back, "Stowmarket Town will win the cup."

Snow White heaved a sigh of relief, thinking "Well, at least Dopey's survived!"

**How many Ipswich** rugby fans does it take to change a light bulb?

None, they're all happy living in Swaffham's shadow!

**Cricket supporters waiting** to watch Sudbury play Great Witchingham heard that the Suffolk team were going to be delayed.

Apparently they saw a sign at the service station that said 'Clean Lavatories'...so they did.

**They say that** a man from Suffolk laughs three times at a joke: the first time when everybody gets it, the second a week later when he thinks he gets it, the third time a month later when somebody explains it to him.

**A man from** Great Yarmouth went into a hardware store and asked to buy a sink.

"Would you like one with a plug?" asked the assistant.

"Don't tell me they've gone electric!" said the man.

**A man from Buxton** bought two horses, but soon realised that he couldn't tell them apart. So he asked the farmer who lived next door what he should do. The farmer suggested measuring them.

The man came back triumphantly and said: "The white horse is two inches taller than the black horse!"

**A man from Cringleford** said to his wife, "Get your coat on love. I'm off to the club".

His wife said, "That's nice. You haven't taken me out for years".

He said, "You're not coming with me...I'm turning the heating off when I go out".

**A vicar from Norfolk** was travelling home one evening and was greatly annoyed when a young man, much the worse for drink, came and sat next to him on the bus.

"Young man," the vicar, declared in a rather pompous tone, "Do you not realise you are on the road to perdition?"

"Oh no!" replied the drunken man, "I could have sworn this bus went to Thetford."

**At an antiques** auction in Holt, a wealthy American announced that he had lost his wallet containing £5,000, and he would give a reward of £50 to the person who found it. From the back of the hall a local man shouted, "I'll give £100!"

NORFOLK Wit & Humour

**Three friends, from UEA,** University Campus Suffolk and Oxford University respectively, were out having a good time together at a funfair. They were just about to go on the helter-skelter when a wise old woman stepped in front of them.

"This is a magic ride," she said. "You will land in whatever you shout out on the way down."

"I'm up for this," said the Norwich student and slid down the helter-skelter shouting "GOLD!" at the top of his voice. Sure enough, when he hit the bottom he found himself surrounded by thousands of pounds worth of gold coins.

The Oxford student went next and shouted "SILVER!" at the top of his voice. At the bottom he landed in more silver coinage than he could carry.

The Suffolk student went last and, launching himself from the top of the slide shouted "WEEEEEEE!".

**A man from Acle** was staggering home one evening, after a heavy night at the pub with his friends.

He suddenly noticed a man from the water board with a big 'T' handle, in the middle of the road opening a valve at the bottom of a manhole.

He walked up behind him and gave him a shove.

"What was that for?" asked the startled man.

The drunken man replied, "That's for turning all the streets round when I'm trying to find my way home!"

**What do you** get if you cross the Newmarket RFU with an OXO cube?

A laughing stock.

**"Suffolk born, Suffolk bred,** strong in the arm and thick in the head!"

Traditional saying

**Two men were** waiting to be served in a butcher's shop. One of them said "I bet you £100 that you can't reach that piece of meat on the ceiling and the other man said "I'm not betting!" The first man replied "Why not?" and the other man answered "The steaks are too high!".

**A farmer from Thetford** was ploughing his field, he looked around and saw the vicar at the gate.

On next his circuit he stopped to say hello.

"My, but you and God have built a beautiful place together" said the vicar.

"You're right, Vicar,' replied the Farmer, "But between you and me, you should have see it when he had it all to himself".

**A life-long career** man, tired of the weekly commute from his home to London, decided he was going to give up his old life and become a chicken farmer. So he bought a chicken farm on the North Norfolk Coast. It turned out that his next door neighbour was also a chicken farmer. The neighbour came for a visit one day and said, "Chicken farming isn't easy you know. To help you get started, I'll give you 100 chickens."

The new chicken farmer was delighted. Two weeks later the neighbour dropped by to see how things were going. The new farmer said, "Not too well mate. All 100 chickens died." The neighbour said, "Oh, I can't believe that. I've never had any trouble with my chickens. I'll give you 100 more." Another two weeks went by and the neighbour dropped in again. The new farmer said, "You're not going to believe this, but the second 100 chickens died too." Astounded, the neighbour asked, "What went wrong?"

The new farmer said, "Well, I'm not sure whether I'm planting them too deep or too close together."

**At a pub in Downham** Market, a newcomer asked a local "Have you lived here all your life?"

After a long pause the man replied "Don't know yet!"

**A tourist in** a shop in North Walsham asked the manager, "Have you got anything in the shape of motor car tyres?" Shopkeeper: "Oh, yes. We've got lifebuoys, funeral wreaths and doughnuts."

**Have you heard** about the latest machine on the beach at Hunstanton?

You put ten pence in and ask it any question and it gives you a true answer.

A holiday maker from Leicester tried it last week.

He asked the machine "Where is my father?" The machine replied:

"Your father is fishing on the Norfolk Broads."

Well, he thought, that's daft for a start because my father is dead.

"Where is my mother's husband?"

The reply came back, "Your mother's husband is buried in Earlham, but your father is still fishing on the Norfolk Broads."

**A man and** his wife walked past a fancy new restaurant in Thorpe St Andrew

... "Did you smell that food?" the woman asked... "Wonderful!"

Being the kind hearted, generous man that he was, her husband thought,

"What the hell, I'll treat her!"

So they walked past it a second time.

**Many years ago** there was a dispute between two villages, one in Norfolk and the other in Suffolk; one day the villagers heard the cry "One Norfolk man is stronger than one hundred Suffolk men."

The villagers in Suffolk were furious and immediately sent their 100 strongest men to engage with the enemy; they were horrified by the screams and shouts. After hours of fighting all was quiet and no-one returned.

Later the same voice shouted out, "Is that the best you can do?"

This fired up the people from Suffolk and they rallied round and got 1000 men to do battle; after days of the most frightful blood curling sounds one man emerged from the battlefield, barely able to speak, but with his last breath managed to murmur "It's a trap, there's two of them!".

**Did you hear** about the truck driver from Framlington who was seen desperately chiselling away at the brickwork after his lorry got stuck at the entrance to a tunnel?

"Why don't you let some air out of your tyres?" asked a helpful passer-by.

"No, mate," replied the driver "It's the roof that won't go under, not the wheels."

**It was a quiet** night in Sprowston and a man and his wife were fast asleep when there was an unexpected knock on the door. The man looked at his alarm clock. It was half past three in the morning. "I'm not getting out of bed at this time," he thought and rolled over.

A louder knock followed. "Aren't you going to answer that?" asked his wife.

So the man dragged himself out of bed and went downstairs. He opened the door to find a strange man standing at the door. It didn't take the homeowner long to realise the man was drunk.

"Hi there," slurred the stranger. "Can you give me a push?"

"No, I'm sorry. It's half past three. I was in bed," said the man and slammed the door. He went back up to bed and told his wife what happened.

"That wasn't very nice of you," she said.

"Remember that night we broke down in the pouring rain on the way to pick the kids up from the babysitter, and you had to knock on that man's door to get us started again? What would have happened if he'd told us to get lost?"

"But the man who just knocked on our door was drunk," replied her husband.

"Well, we can at least help move his car somewhere safe and sort him out a taxi," said his wife. "He needs our help." So the husband got out of bed again, got dressed, and went downstairs. He opened the door, but couldn't to see the stranger anywhere so he shouted, "Hey, do you still want a push?". In answer, he heard a voice call out, "Yes please!" So, still being unable to see the stranger, he shouted,

"Where are you?"

"I'm over here," the stranger replied, "on your swing."

**Did you hear** about the last wish of the henpecked husband of a house-proud wife?

He asked to have his ashes scattered on the carpet.

**There are many** good things to come out of Suffolk - most of them roads leading to Norfolk.

**Two blokes from Norwich** went into a pub.

The first man said "A pint o' bitter, and a half o' shandy for my mate 'Donkey', please!"

The publican replied "'What's with him calling you 'Donkey'?"

The second one said "Oh, 'e aw, 'e aw, 'e always calls me that!"

**A farmer was** driving along a country road near Taverham with a large load of fertiliser. A little boy, playing in front of his house, saw him and called, "What do you have on your truck?"

"Fertiliser," the farmer replied.

"What are you going to do with it?" asked the little boy.

"Put it on strawberries," answered the farmer.

"You ought to live here," the little boy advised him. 'We put sugar and cream on ours."

**Pete and Larry** hadn't seen each other in many years. They were having a long chat, telling each other all about their lives. Finally Pete invited Larry to visit him in his new flat in Wroxham. "I have a wife and three kids and I'd love to have you visit us."

"Great. Where do you live?"

"Here's the address. There's plenty of parking behind the flat. Park and come around to the front door, kick it open with your foot, go to the elevator and press the button with your left elbow, then enter! When you reach the sixth floor, go down the hall until you see my name on the door. Then press the doorbell with your right elbow and I'll let you in."

"Great. But tell me…what is all this business of kicking the front door open, then pressing elevator buttons with my right, then my left elbow?"

Pete answered, "Surely you're not coming empty-handed?"

**Sam worked in** an office in Norwich. One day he walked into his boss's office and said, "I'll be honest with you, I know the economy isn't great, but I have three companies after me, and I would like to respectfully ask for a pay rise."

After a few minutes of haggling, his manager finally agreed to a 5% pay rise, and Sam happily got up to leave.

"By the way", asked the boss as Sam got up, "Which three companies are after you?"

"The electric company, the water company, and the phone company", Sam replied.

**A man from Swaffham** wanted to become a monk so he went to the monastery and talked to the head monk.

The head monk said, "You must take a vow of silence and can only say two words every three years."

The man agreed and after the first three years, the head monk came to him and said, "What are your two words?"

"Food cold!" the man replied.

Three more years went by and the head monk came to him and said "What are your two words?"

"Robe dirty!" the man exclaimed.

Three more years went by and the head monk came to him and said, "What are your two words?"

"I quit!" said the man.

"Well", the head monk replied, "I'm not surprised. You've done nothing but complain ever since you got here!"

**A lawyer from Suffolk** and a businessman from Norfolk ended up sitting next to each other on a long haul flight to Stanstead.

The lawyer started thinking that he could have some fun at the businessman's expense and asked him if he'd like to play a game. The businessman was tired and just wanted to relax. He politely declined the offer and tried to sleep. The lawyer persisted, explaining:

"I ask you a question, and if you don't know the answer, you pay me only £5; you ask me one, and if I don't know the answer, I will pay you £500."

This got the Norfolk man a little more interested and he finally agreed to play the game.

The lawyer asked the first question, "What's the distance from the Earth to the moon?"

The businessman said nothing, but reached into his pocket, pulled out a five-pound note and handed it to the lawyer.

Now, it was his turn to ask the questions. He asked the lawyer, "What goes up a hill with three legs, and comes down with four?"

The lawyer used his laptop. He used the air-phone; he searched the web, he sent emails to his most well read friends, but still came up with nothing. After over an hour of searching, he finally gave up.

He woke up the businessman and handed him £500. The man smugly pocketed the cash and went straight back to sleep.

The lawyer went wild with curiosity and wanted to know the answer. He woke the Norfolk man up and asked, "Well? What goes up a hill with three legs and comes down with four?"

The man reached into his pocket, handed the lawyer £5 and went back to sleep.

**Two elderly ladies** were enjoying a half pint of shandy in a pub in Dereham. One said to the other, "Was it love at first sight when you met your old man?"" No I don't think so," came the reply,"I didn't know 'ow much money he had when I first met him!"

**Jack from Attleborough** got onto the bus with his hands held out in front of him about a foot apart. The conductor came up to him and said, "Give us your fare, Jack!" "I can't" replied Jack. "I'll pay you on the way back." The conductor looked puzzled and said, "I'll get the sack if the inspector gets on. I've got to have your fare now!". "That's nothing to what I'll get when I go home" reasoned Jack "And I have to tell the missus to re measure the window I bust this morning!"

**A bloke walked** up to the foreman of a road laying gang in North Norfolk and asked for a job. "I haven't got one for you today." said the foreman looking up from his newspaper. "But if you walk half a mile down here, you can see if you like the work and I can put you on the list for tomorrow."That's great mate," said the bloke as he wandered off down the road to find the gang. At the end of the shift, the man walked past the foreman and shouted, "Thanks mate. See you tomorrow." The foreman looked up from his paper and shouted back, "You've enjoyed yourself then?" "Yes I have!" shouted back the bloke, "But can I have a shovel or a pick to lean on like the rest of the gang?"

**A labourer shouted** up to his roofer mate on top of an old terraced house in Aylsham, saying, "Don't start climbing down this ladder, Burt." "Why not?" Burt called back. "Cos I moved it five minutes ago!" replied his mate.

**A school pupil** from Bowthorpe asked his teacher, "Are 'trousers' singular or plural?"

The teacher replied, "They're singular on top and plural on the bottom."

**A visitor from Suffolk** was driving around Sheringham in his fancy new car and found that he was lost. The driver stopped old Tom and said, "You there! Old man, what happens if I turn left here?" "Don't know sir," replied old Tom.

"Well what if I turn right here, where will that take me?" continued the visitor. "Don't know sir." replied old Tom. Becoming exasperated, the driver

continued, "Well, what if I go straight on?" A flicker of knowledge moved over old Tom's face until he replied, "Don't know sir." "I say old man you don't know a lot do you?" retorted the posh bloke. Old Tom looked at him and said, "I may not know a lot but I ain't lost like you are!" With that, old Tom walked off leaving the motorist stranded.

**Harry proudly drove** his new convertible into town and parked it on the main street he was on his way to the recycling centre to get rid of an unwanted gift, a foot spa, which he left on the back seat.

He had walked half way down the street when he realised that he had left the top down... with the foot spa in the back.

He ran all the way back to his car, but it was too late...

Another five foot spas had been dumped in the car.

**What gear were** you in at the moment of the impact?
Gucci sweats and Reeboks.

**Two aerials meet** on a roof - fall in love - get married. The
ceremony was rubbish - but the reception was brilliant.

**A duck walks** into a pub and goes up to the barman.

The barman says 'What can I get you?'

Duck: 'Umm. Do you have any grapes?'

Barman (Looking surprised):

'No, I'm afraid we don't.'

The duck waddles slowly out of the pub.

The next day at the same time, the duck waddles into the pub, hops up on a bar stool.

Barman: 'Hi. What can I get for you?'

Duck: 'Um. Do you have any grapes?'

Barman (a little annoyed): 'Hey! Weren't you in here yesterday. Look mate, we don't have any grapes. OK?'

The duck hops off the stool and waddles out of the door.

The next day, at the same time, the barman is cleaning some glasses when he hears a familiar voice

Duck: 'Umm.. Do you have any grapes?'

The barman is really annoyed

Barman: 'Look. What's your problem? You came in here yesterday asking for grapes, I told you, we don't have any grapes! Next time I see your little ducktail waddle in here I'm going to nail those little webbed feet of yours to the floor. GOT me pal?'

So the duck hops off the bar stool and waddles out.

The next day at the same time, the duck waddles into the pub, walks up to the barman and the barman says,

'What on earth do YOU want?'

'Errrr. do you have any nails?'

'What!? Of course not.'

'Oh. Well, do you have any grapes?'

**A new client** had just come in to see a famous lawyer.

'Can you tell me how much you charge?', said the client.

'Of course', the lawyer replied, 'I charge £200 to answer three questions!'

'Well that's a bit steep, isn't it?'

'Yes it is,' said the lawyer, 'And what's your third question?'

**A passenger in** a taxi tapped the driver on the shoulder to ask him something.

The driver screamed, lost control of the cab, nearly hit a bus, drove up

over the curb and stopped just inches from a large plate glass window.

For a few moments everything was silent in the cab, then the driver said, 'Please, don't ever do that again. You scared the daylights out of me.'

The passenger, who was also frightened, apologised and said he didn't realize that a tap on the shoulder could frighten him so much, to which the driver replied, 'I'm sorry, it's really not your fault at all. Today is my first day driving a cab. I've been driving a hearse for the last 25 years.'

**The leader of** a vegetarian society just couldn't control himself any more. He simply needed to try some pork, just to see what it tasted like. So one day he told his members he was going away for a break. He left town and headed to the nearest restaurant. After sitting down, he ordered a roasted pig, and impatiently waited for his treat. After just a few minutes, he heard someone call his name, and to his horror he saw one of his fellow members walking towards him. Just at that same moment, the waiter walked over, with a huge platter, holding a full roasted pig with an apple in its mouth. 'Isn't that something,' says the man after only a moment's pause, 'All I do is order an apple, and look what it comes with!'

**Phil's nephew came** to him with a problem. 'I have my choice of two women,' he said, 'A beautiful, penniless young girl whom I love dearly, and a rich widow whom I can't stand.'

'Follow your heart; marry the girl you love,' Phil counselled.

'Very well, Uncle Phil,' said the nephew, 'That's sound advice.'

'By the way,' asked Phil 'Where does the widow live?'

**A high-rise** building was going up in Norwich, three steel erectors sat on a girder having their lunch. 'Oh, no, not cream cheese and walnut again', said the Arthur first 'If I get the same again tomorrow, I'll jump off the girder.'

Harry opened his packet. 'Oh, no, not a Caesar salad with salami and lettuce on rye,' he said. 'If I get the same again tomorrow, I'll jump off too.'

Orson, the third man, opened his lunch. 'Oh, no, not another potato sandwich,' he said. 'If I get the same again tomorrow, I'll follow you two off the girder.'

The next day, Arthur got cream cheese and walnut. Without delay, he jumped. Harry saw he had Caesar salad with salami and lettuce on rye. With a wild cry, he too leapt. The third man then opened his lunchbox. 'Oh, no,' he said. 'Potato sandwiches.' And he too jumped.

The foreman, who had overheard their conversation, reported what had happened, and the funerals were held together.

'If only I'd known,' sobbed Arthur's wife.

'If only he'd said,' wailed Harry's.

'I don't understand it at all,' said Orson's wife. 'He always got his own sandwiches ready.'

**Ian was having** a pint at his local when a loud mouthed guy called Henry walked in. Ian couldn't help overhearing Henry trying to bet a couple of young lads 50 quid that they couldn't drink 20 pints in 20 minutes. After a lot of cajoling, Henry was unsuccessful in his goal to make a few quid. He looked around at Ian and said 'Well what about you then? Are you game?' Ian shrugged, downed his pint and left the pub.

Half an hour later Ian walked back into his local and said to Henry 'I'll take that bet.' Sure enough Henry smiled at the easy money he would make as Ian began to drink the pints. Henry's smile soon disappeared when Ian polished off the 20 pints in 19 minutes. Handing over the cash, Henry said 'When you left the here earlier, where did you go?' Ian looked at him and replied 'I had to go to the pub down the road to see if I could do it first.'

**A couple from Norwich** had been courting for nearly twenty years. One day as they sat on a seat in the park, the woman plucked up the courage to ask,

"Don't you think it's time we got married?"

Her sweetheart answered,

"Yes, but who'd have us?"

**A teacher at** a school in Sherringham; was having a little trouble getting her year 11 pupils to understand grammar, 'These are what we call the pronouns', she said, 'And this is how we use them with verbs; I am, you are, he/she is' she was saying, to glazed looks.

Trying a different tack she said, Lauren, give me a sentence with the pronoun, 'I' in it.'

Lauren began, 'I is...'

'No, no, no, no, no NO, NO!', shouted the teacher, 'Never, 'I is', always, 'I am'... now try again'.

Lauren looked puzzled and a little hurt, thought a while then began again more quietly,'I... am...the ninth letter of the alphabet'.